Animals
That Help Us

Dogs

Jean Coppendale

QED Publishing

Words in **bold** can be found in the Glossary on page 23.

Copyright © QED Publishing 2007

First published in the UK in 2007 by
QED Publishing
A Quarto Group company
226 City Road
London EC1V 2TT
www.qed-publishing.co.uk

A catalogue record for this book is available from the British Library.

ISBN 978 1 84538 666 5

Written by Jean Coppendale
Designed by Melissa Alaverdy
Editor Paul Manning

Publisher Steve Evans
Creative Director Zeta Davies
Senior Editor Hannah Ray

Picture credits

Alamy: p8 bl Jack Sullivan; p8-9 Shout; p10-11 Mike Abrahams; p13 ct tom Kidd. Corbis: contents page Jim Richardson; p4 bl & p22 cc Jim Craigmyle; front cover & p4-5: LWA-Sharie Kennedy/zefa; p6-7, p7 br Paul A.Souders; p10 bl Daemmrich Bob/Sygma; p11 tr & p22 cl Ruben Sprich/Reuters; p12-13: Owen Franken; p14-15: Alison Wright; p15 ct Layne Kennedy; p22-23 Beat Glanzman/zefa. Dogs for the Disabled: p20 bl. Getty Images: p11 tr: Erik S. Lesser/Stringer. Guide Dogs: title page; p16-17. Rex Features: p18-19: EDP Pics/K. Tovell; p20-21.Vivid Sync./www.hearingdogs.org.uk: p18 bl.

Printed and bound in China

Contents

How dogs help us

Dogs help us in many different ways. They help farmers look after sheep and **cattle**. They work with the police to keep us safe and help to find people who are lost. Some dogs are trained to help people with **physical disabilities**, and pet dogs give us love and friendship.

Working dogs are loyal and often become very close to their owners.

With the right care
and lots of love,
a dog will be your
friend for life.

5

Dogs on the farm

For hundreds of years, dogs have worked on farms, helping farmers to look after their animals. Sheep dogs are used to round up sheep on the hills and in the fields. When all the sheep are together, the dogs will guide them back to the farm or into another field.

These sheepdogs are working as a team to keep the sheep under control.

6

Some **breeds** are better at doing certain jobs. This dog is good at working with cattle.

Tracker dogs

Dogs have a very strong sense of smell, and police dogs are trained to use this to track down **criminals** and missing persons.

Policemen and women who work with dogs are called dog-handlers.

Before they do this, they must first pick up the **scent** by sniffing something that belongs to the person, such as a handkerchief or a piece of clothing.

A tracker dog will follow the scent trail through the countryside, over fields and through woods – wherever it may lead.

Sniffer dogs

Specially trained dogs are often used at airports, railway stations and other public places to sniff out anything dangerous or **illegal**. When a sniffer dog smells something it has been trained to search for, it will scratch at the ground or bark until its handler comes to see what it has found.

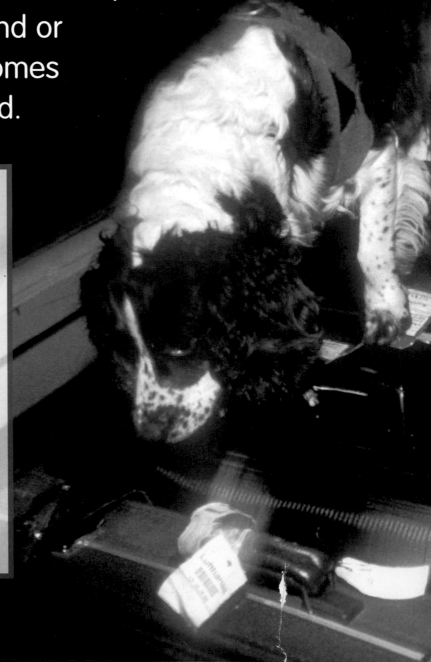

A sniffer dog and its handler both crouch down to search for stolen goods hidden underneath a car.

King's Cross

A policeman and a sniffer dog on duty at a busy station in London.

Rescue dogs

If a building collapses in an accident or earthquake, dogs are used to find survivors who may be trapped underneath the rubble. The dogs try to pick up the scent of trapped people. They also use their excellent hearing to listen for anyone calling out. Then they bark to alert the rescue workers.

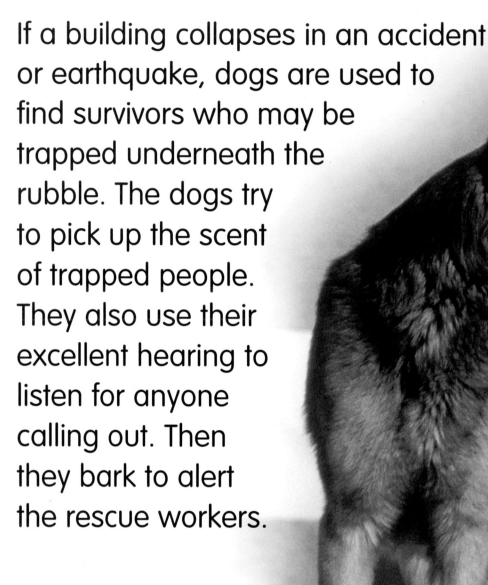

Dogs like this are often first on the scene after an accident or **natural disaster**.

Dogs are also trained to rescue climbers and walkers who are lost or injured in the mountains. This dog's special jacket means it can be seen in bad weather.

Snow dogs

Huskies are dogs that live in very cold countries and help people by **herding** reindeer and pulling sledges. One husky is strong enough to pull a small sledge on its own. On long journeys, teams of huskies take turns to pull sledges across the ice. Sometimes huskies will travel for several days through snow and icy winds.

This husky is wearing special boots to protect its paws from ice and cold.

Using a sledge pulled by a team of huskies can be a good, fast way to travel from place to place in bad weather conditions.

Guide dogs

Guide dogs are specially trained to work with people who are blind or **partially sighted** and to help them with their daily lives. The dogs take their owners everywhere – to and from work, to the shops and to visit friends. They are also trained to help their owners to get on and off buses and trains, and to cross busy roads.

Only dogs that are gentle and enjoy being with people are chosen to be guide dogs.

Guide dogs must start their training at an early age to learn all the skills they will need.

Hearing dogs

Hearing dogs are special helpers for people who are deaf or who have hearing problems. When the dog hears the doorbell or some other noise, it will touch its owner gently with its paw to tell them that something is happening. The dogs can also be trained to make different signs for different noises.

As well as practical help, hearing dogs give their owners friendship, love and enjoyment.

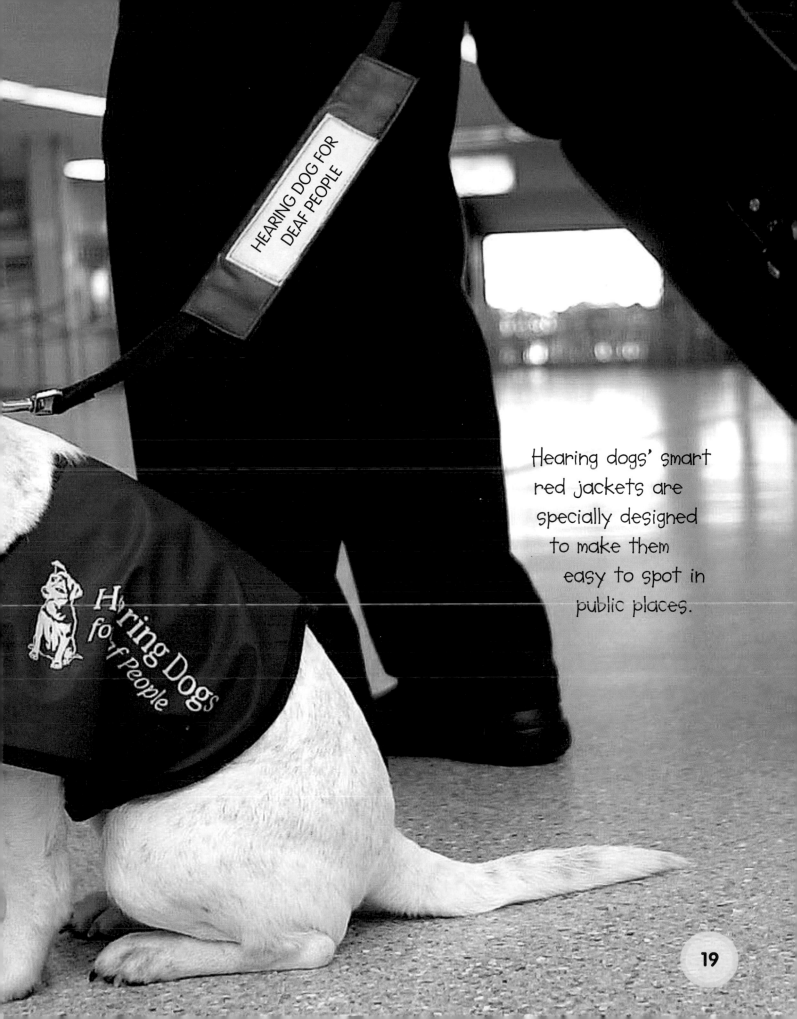

HEARING DOG FOR DEAF PEOPLE

Hearing Dogs for Deaf People

Hearing dogs' smart red jackets are specially designed to make them easy to spot in public places.

Dogs for the disabled

Assistance dogs live with people who have a physical disability or who have to use a wheelchair. These dogs can do lots of jobs for their owners. They can open doors, pick up dropped items, carry bags and even switch lights on and off.

For a wheelchair-user, everyday tasks can be very difficult. This dog is helping its owner get a box of breakfast cereal out of the kitchen cupboard.

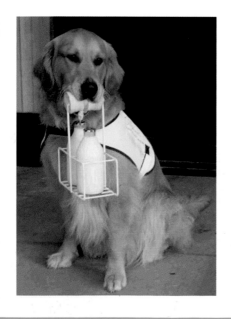

Many assistance dogs are 'rescue' dogs. These are dogs that were once abandoned or badly treated by unkind people. Their new owners are glad to have them and look after them well.

Activities

- Which is your favourite working dog? Why? Write about a day in its life. Describe what it does.

- Look at these pictures of two dogs from the book. Which one is the police dog? What does the other dog do?

- Draw or paint a picture of your favourite working dog. Write a sentence about what the dog does underneath the picture.

- Choose a time for dog-spotting. During this time, make a note of any working dogs you see on the streets, on television or in books and magazines. Which dog did you spot most often?

Glossary

assistance dogs
dogs who give special help to a person who is disabled

breed
type of dog such as a poodle or Alsatian

cattle
cows that are kept on a farm or ranch

criminals
people who have committed a crime and broken the law

herding
rounding up sheep or cattle and moving them somewhere new, such as a field

illegal
when something is against the law

natural disaster
a large accident or emergency caused by nature, such as an earthquake

partially sighted
when somebody cannot see very well

physical disability
something wrong with part of your body that stops you doing something

scent
special smell that only a dog can recognize

Index